LEARNING ITALIAN ACAD

ITALIAN SHORT STORIES FOR BEGINNERS

Become Fluent in Less Than 30 Days
Using a Proven Scientific Method Applied in These Language Lessons.
Practice Vocabulary, Conversation & Grammar Daily
(series 1)

Table of Contents

Introduction

Welcome to "Italian Short Stories for Beginners: Learn Italian for Beginners with 50 Short Stories to Learn Italian Language, Growing your Vocabulary for a better Italian". In this book, you will find a collection of short stories that will help you get a head start on learning Spanish in a quick and simple fashion.

Learning Italian, like any other language, can be a challenging task. But it doesn't have to more challenging than it needs to. In fact, most books, methods and courses out there guarantee results in a short period of time. However, they don't take the time to present learners with the fundamentals that will enable them to make the most of their learning experience.

That is why this book is focused on providing you with the fundamentals that you will need in order to learn Spanish for the first time, or to brush up on your current skills. After all, why not make the most of your time and effort by learning another language?

As a matter of fact, being able to speak a foreign language, not to mention multiple languages, is a skill which is always in demand. While you may not actually get a job based on your linguistic competence alone, your ability to speak other languages will set you apart from anyone else in the business world.

What is you are keen on learning Italian because you would like to travel? Then we've got you covered, too. You can take these lessons as a means of getting a grasp on the fundamentals that you will need in order to navigate your way through Italian-speaking countries. If you are learning Italian because you are looking to take on a new challenge, then by all means, go right ahead and take advantage of this opportunity to do so.

The fact of the matter is that learning Italian doesn't have to be an overwhelming task. With the tips, techniques and strategies that we will outline in this book, you will have a very good sense of how you can go about using the lessons contained herein to improve your Italian skills. Furthermore, you will be able to learn how to learn any language as the tips, techniques and strategies can be applied to virtually any language out there.

So, what are you waiting for?

The longer you wait to take on this challenge, the longer it will take you to achieve your goal of speaking another language. Whether Italian is your second language, or your third, fourth, fifth, and so on, you will find the content in this book easy to manage. As such, you won't have to work harder than you have to. You will have the right tools to achieve your goals in the shortest amount of time possible.

Please bear in mind that there is one essential ingredient in learning Italian, or any language for that matter: consistency. Please make the effort to be consistent in your endeavors to learn this wonderful language. You will find that consistency will make things a lot easier for you.

See you on the inside.

SECTION I:

Fundamentals of Learning Italian

Chapter 1:
Tips and Strategies for Learning Italian

In this chapter, we will be taking a look at useful tips, techniques and strategies which you can use to learn Italian. As a matter of fact, the information contained in this chapter can be easily extrapolated to the learning of any language and not just Italian. As such, you can feel confident that the content in this chapter is applicable well beyond this book.

For most folks, learning a language can seem like a daunting task. The main reason behind this lies in the fact that most folks are unfamiliar with the dynamic of learning a language. Consequently, they don't really know where to begin and how to make the most of their efforts.

Hence, many language learners tend to quit after a while because they can't seem to gain enough traction. This leads to frustration as struggling with a new language is never a pleasant experience. However, much of the frustration and struggles can be avoided by learning the ropes of how languages work.

The underpinnings of any language lie in the way the language is structured. In the case of Italian, its basis lies in the conjugation of verbs. This means that you must become familiar with the various verb conjugations in order to fully understand how to structure the various verb tenses used throughout the language.

This can be a bit complicated with Romance languages. So, French, Spanish, Italian, Portuguese and Romanian receive the denomination of "Romance" languages since they are mainly derived from Latin which was the language of the old Roman Empire.

Over the centuries, each one of these languages has acquired its own nuances that make it unique. While they all have the same underpinnings, the visible surface can be quite different. Thus, it is important to get a firm understanding of how these languages work.

In this book, we will predominantly focus on the present tense as it is the most widely used tense in the Italian language. Most Italian speakers tend to use what are known as "simple" tenses since they tend to focus on just one tense at a time.

This is a stark contrast to the English language as most English speakers are able to weave their way in and out of various verb tenses. This can make conversation rather complex especially when topics warrant the use of several verb tenses.

The starting point with the Italian language lies with the infinitive form of verbs. Verbs that do not have a verb tense are known as "infinitives". In other words, this is their pure form prior to being conjugated into a specific verb tense. In English, the infinitive form of verbs is written out as "to play" for example.

In Italian, the infinitive form of verbs is defined by the ending of each verb. As such, there are three main forms in which infinitive verbs end. This is what will become the basis of the conjugation for each verb.

The other factor that will determine the manner in which a verb must be conjugated is the subject of the sentence. This is exactly the same as English. As such, depending on the subject that agrees with the verb, the verb must be conjugated in a specific manner.

So, let's take a look at the subject pronouns which can be used in Spanish.

Io (I)

Tu (you, singular)

Egli(he, masculine)

Ella (she, feminine)

Noi (we)

Voi (you, plural)

Essi (they, masculine)

Esse (they, feminine)

This list above presents the subject pronouns which are used in the Italian language. Thus, this opens the door for a couple of important aspects to consider.

First, you will notice that there is a singular and a plural "you". In English, "you" is used to refer to both singular and plural nouns. So, "you are a teacher" and "you are teachers" use the same subject pronoun though its function is different.

Please note that English is an outlier in this regard as virtually all languages make a distinction between the singular and plural versions of "you". As such, it is important to keep this mind as you navigate throughout the texts and conversation you find in Italian.

Another important distinction between English and most other languages, especially Romance languages, is the use of the masculine and feminine for nouns. English is a gender-neutral language. What this means is that nouns do not receive a "male" or "female" denomination. Nouns are simply referred to in a single, genderless tone.

Italian assigns a gender to all nouns. This might get a bit tricky as determining which nouns are masculine and which nouns are feminine can be tough. But rest assured that with practice and experience, you will be able to get a firm grasp on this. We will be taking a deeper look at this in the next chapter.

One other fundamental difference between Romance languages and English is the various ways in which you can address a person. In Italian, there are two main forms in which you can address a person. The most common form is "tu". This form is an informal "you". It can be used to address people of a similar age, station or friends, family and other acquaintances with whom you have a high degree of familiarity.

In the case of "voi", this is the formal version of "you". This form is used to refer to people who are much older than you, have a higher station, such as an employer, or people with whom you are not very familiar, for example, new acquaintances whom you've just met.

With these fundamentals in mind, let's take a look at learning strategies which you can use throughout this book.

Consistency is the biggest success factor you will encounter when learning a language. Regardless of whether you can devote 15 minutes, or 2 hours a day, the most important thing to keep in mind is that a consistent amount of time dedicated to learning will go a long way.

In this regard, most folks "binge learn", that is, they will not touch their books for days and then spend hours on end trying to make the time. Think about it along these lines: imagine you do not go to the gym for a week and then you decide to spend 3 hours working out on a Saturday morning. What do you think the result of that would be?

The same principle applies to language learning.

Repetition is another success factor. When you go over your lessons multiple times, you will be able to better fixate information and knowledge into your mind. After all, humans are not built to learn things instantaneously. Humans need practice and repetition before they can master any skill. That same concept applies to language. The more practice you get, the more your skills will improve.

Keep a learning diary. Keeping a learning diary, or a log of your activities, will help you visualize what you are doing to help yourself learn. In other words, you are keeping track of your language learning tasks. What this does is help you to see what works and doesn't. Later on, you can always refer back to those tasks which are providing you with the most value and which ones are not.

Making handwritten notes will help fixate knowledge much better. Of course, using your phone, laptop or tablet makes life a lot easier. However, making handwritten notes enables the brain to involve more senses in the learning process. As such, individual words and grammar will permeate your mind in such a way that the mechanics of grammar, word order and spelling become clear in your mind.

Use a tool such as http://www.oneworditaliano.com/ as a grammar and conjugation reference. In addition, this tool will also provide you with the pronunciation of words. Consequently, you will have a tool that can support you when you are working on your own. Furthermore, it is a great study tool or just serve as a reference when you are curious about something related to your Italian lessons.

Now, let's look at a suggested methodology which you can use to help you get the most out of this book. Of course, this is not the only way that you can take advantage of the material in this book. Nevertheless, this methodology is designed to help you utilize the contents of this book to the fullest.

- Firstly, read each story once, all the way through. At first, it will be hard to make sense of its contents. However, as you go through the story, you will see some words which resemble English words. These words, most of the time, will basically be the same English word. For example, "responsable" and "responsible" resemble each other almost identically. And yes, they have the same meaning. Consider this: "police" and "policía". It is practically the same word. So, you can highlight, or underline, these words and make note of them.

- Next, go through the text a second time. You will see your comprehension improving significantly. You will notice how similar-looking and sounding words make the text a lot easier to understand.

- After, go through the text highlighting, or underlining, words which are completely unfamiliar to you. Hopefully they won't be that many, but there will be some of these words. This will help you to visualize how much of the vocabulary is actually new to you.

- Then, you can use a tool such as http://www.oneworlditaliano.com/ or www.wordreference.com to help you find the meaning, pronunciation and usage of these new vocabulary items.

- Once you have found translations, synonyms and equivalent meanings, you can then proceed to run through the entire text one more time. You will find that the text is now much more comprehensible that it once was. This will enable you to make greater sense of the content in each lesson.

- After you feel comfortable with the language in the lesson, you can proceed to the questions located at the end of the lesson. The questions are intended to help you gain further practice into question formation, word order and reading comprehension. The questions have been designed to be open-ended. As such, there is no single way of answering. Nevertheless, we have taken care to provide suggested responses in order to provide you with guidance.

- Once you feel confident in answering each question, you go back and give the text one more run through. You can read the text aloud for further practice. If you are shy about your pronunciation, pick a time when you are alone and go through it.

- If you so choose, you can use a tool such as the Text to Speech plugin for Google Chrome to read the text for you. This will give you a great sense of how the text is pronounced. As such, you will be able to get the perfect pronunciation and thereby help you get the right pronunciation as well.

- One good tip is to have a vocabulary notebook. You can use your learning journal to write down all of the vocabulary words which you encounter on a daily basis. What this enables you to do is to keep track of all the new words that you learn on a given day. Thus, the act of writing things down by hand will help to further fixate ideas in your mind.

- Lastly, watching Italian language content on television or online will also help you to practice your listening skills while allowing you to learn more vocabulary and grammar. So, do try to make the most of the opportunities around to improve your Italian skills.

With these tips and strategies, you will be well on your way to improving your overall Italian skills. In the next chapter we will be taking a closer look at language aspects which tend to be particularly tricky for English speakers.

Chapter 2:
Common Problems when Learning Italian

In this chapter, we are going to be looking at the various problem areas that English speakers generally tend to have when they seek out to learn Italian. As such, we will be going over them in this chapter so as to provide insight and recommendations on how to deal with them as you progress through your Italian learning endeavors.

Earlier, we established that Spanish, just like French and Italian, is a Romance language. In contrast, English is of Germanic origin. What this means is that English and Spanish were born in different neighborhood. Nevertheless, they do have one, common thread: French.

The influence of French upon the English language has led it to have some striking similarities with Italian. However, there are enough difference between both languages to throw a monkey wrench into anyone's learning endeavors.

What does this mean?

It means that when English speakers go about learning Spanish, they will run into some essential differences that will be challenging at first, but don't necessarily have to insurmountable. As such, it is important to understand these differences in order to make them more accessible to learners.

The first big difference is gender.

Gender tends to be one of the biggest sources of frustration to Italian learners as there is no clear rule or guideline to determine which objects are masculine and which ones are feminine. The easiest way to identify gender among nouns is by observing the article that precedes it.

For example, "il" is used for masculine and "la" is used for feminine. So, "il sole" (the sun) is masculine whereas "la luna" is feminine. This is a good rule of thumb to follow when you are reading a text or simply hearing regular conversation.

However, it gets tricky when you see, or think, of an object but you are unaware of the article that precedes it. In this case, it can be tough to figure out the gender of an object. Since there really is no way to determine this just by looking at the object itself, there is one way in which you can figure this out: look at the object's name.

In general, the names of masculine nouns end in "o" and feminine nouns end in "a". This is a good rule of thumb to follow as the endings will help you to figure out their gender.

For instance, these are some examples of masculine nouns:

Ragazzo (boy)

Palo (stick)

Letto (bed)

As you can see, these nouns are all masculine given their endings. Also, there are some exceptions which you can keep an eye out for. Nouns that end in "ma" and "pa" are masculine. For example, "mapa" (map) and "problema" (problem) are masculine.

Regarding feminine nouns, the general rule of thumb is that they end in an "a". Here are some examples:

Scimmia (monkey)

Casa (house)

Pianta (plant)

Mamma (mother)

Foglia (leaf)

As you can see, these are feminine nouns based on the fact that they end in "a". However, there are some exceptions as always. Nouns that end in "ione" such as "relazione" (relation), "izia" such as "Amicizia" (friendship) and "esta" such as "richiesta" (request) are considered feminine.

Also, another good rule of thumb is that nouns can be converted into feminine by adding an "essa" or an "a" to it. For instance, "dottore" which is masculine, can become feminine as "dottoressa". Also, "infermiere" (nurse, male) would become "infermiera" (nurse, female) by simply substituting the "o" for the "a" ending.

Also, there are a couple of interesting exceptions:

- La mano (hand) is feminine despite ending in an "o".
- La radio (the radio) is feminine despite ending in an "o".
- La notte (night) is also feminine.

Please keep in mind that Italian always uses the articles "el" and "la" to precede the reference to a noun. Conversely, English does not use this form unless the speaker is being specific about the noun in question.

With this guide, you can begin to navigate your way through the world of masculine and feminine nouns. As you gain more practice and experience, you will find that it is actually rather straightforward. So, do take the time to go over them.

Another area to take into consideration is verb conjugation.

Unlike English, Spanish has a specific verb conjugation for verbs based on the subject that it agrees with and the verb tense.

This is rather simple and straightforward in the English language as verb conjugation does not necessarily imply radically modifying the verb's structure. However, Italian does require verb endings to be changed in accordance to the subject it agrees with. But fear not, we will make this very straightforward.

The first thing to look out for the ending of the verb in its infinitive form. As stated earlier, the infinitive form of a verb is when it has not been conjugated to agree with a subject in a particular verb tense. as such, the infinitive form of the verb is key in order to determine how it will be conjugated.

Verbs in the infinitive form in Italian will end in one of three ways: "are", "ere" and "ire". So, let's take a look at some examples of this:

Verbs ending in "are"

Giocare (to play)

Viaggiare (to travel)

Cantare (to sing)

Firmare (to sign)

Now, let's take a look at some verbs that end in "ere":

Verbs ending in "ere":

Essere (to be)

Correre (to run)

Risolvere (to solve)

Rispondere (to respond)

Here is a list of some verbs ending in "ire":

Verbs ending in "ire"

Aprire (to open)

Coprire (to cover)

Sentire (to feel)

The above examples are a small sample size of the verbs which you will encounter throughout your study of the Italian language. As such, let's take a look at how these verbs are conjugated in the present simple tense.

Here is a chart which explains the various endings for each subject and according to the verb ending.

Subject pronoun	ARE	ERE	IRE
Io(I)	o	o	o
Tu(you, singular)	ai	ei	i
Egli(he)	a	e	e
Ella (she)	a	e	e
Noi (we)	iamo	iamo	iamo
Voi (you, plural)	ate	iete	ite
Essi (they, masculine)	no	no	no
Esse (they, feminine)	no	no	no

Figure 1. Verb endings in the present simple tense.

The chart above show the endings that are to be attached depending on the subject that a verb will agree with. Hence, let's take a look at some examples in order to make this point evident.

Infinitive: cantare (to sing)

Io canto (I sing)

Tu canti (you sing, singular)

Egli canta (he sings)

Ella canta (she sings)

Noi cantiamo (we sing)

Voi cantate (you sing, plural)

Essi cantano (they sing, masculine)

Esse cantano (they sing, feminine)

As you can see, the original "are" ending is dropped in favor of the corresponding ending based on the subject. With the exception of a handful of irregular verbs, this is the rule of thumb to follow with verbs ending in "are".

Consequently, the same pattern applies to the verbs ending in "ere" and "ire". Let's have a look at some examples.

Infinitive: vivere (to live)

Io vivo (I live)

Tu vivi (you live, singular)

Egli vive (he lives)

Ella vive (she lives)

Noi viviamo (we live)

Voi vivete (you live, plural)

Essi vivono (they live, masculine)

Esse vivono (they live, feminine)

As with the "ar" verbs, the "ir" ending is dropped in favor of the corresponding ending. Let's take a look at an example of an "ire" verb.

Infinitive: dormire (to sleep)

Io dormo (I sleep)

Tu dormi (you sleep, singular)

Egli dorme (he sleeps)

Ella dorme (she sleeps)

Noi dormiamo (we sleep)

Voi dormite (you sleep, plural)

Essi dormono (they sleep, masculine)

Esse dormono (they sleep, feminine)

Given the previous examples, the conjugation of verbs in the present simple are rather straightforward. Of course, it takes some time and practice. Nevertheless, you can become proficient with verb conjugations in a relatively short period of time. As such, all you need is to dedicate some time and effort in to practicing the way verbs are to be conjugated. If you are ever in doubt, http://www.oneworlditaliano.com/ is a great tool which you can consult in order to get the right conjugation.

On other significant difference between English and Italian is the use of subjects, or lack thereof, in sentences. In Italian it is quite common to omit the use of a subject at the beginning of sentence especially when it is clear who is being referred to in the conversation. As such, speakers will often take the liberty of omitting the subject observing only the proper conjugation of the verb.

Needless to say, this can cause confusion even among native Italian speakers. The reason for this is that unless there is a clear understanding of who is being referred to, it can be very difficult to keep track of a conversation.

Let's look at an example:

Sono degli Stati Uniti (I am from the United States).

In this example, the use of the from "sono" (am) is the proper conjugation for the verb "essere" (to be) in the present simple tense. However, it is rather clear that "sono" refers to "I am", hence, a Italian speaker would be more than willing to dump "io" (I) give the fact that it is perfectly clear that this individual is referring to themselves.

So, do keep an eye out for this type of omission as you will frequently see it throughout the text presented in this book.

Let's look at the conjugation of "essere":

Infinitive: essere (to be)

Io sono (I am)

Tu sei (you are, singular)

Egli è (he is)

Ella è (she is)

Noi siamo (we are)

Voi siete (you are, plural)

Essi sono (they are, masculine)

Esse sono (they are, feminine)

Please note that "essere" is irregular as the base form of the verb changes in order to accommodate its corresponding ending as an "ere" verb.

With this, we have laid the groundwork for the content in this book. We are now ready to move on to the short stories prepared for your study. Please keep in mind that nothing is ever cast in stone when it comes to language. Nevertheless, the patterns which we have laid out herein will provide you with a good head start when it comes to improving your Spanish skills.

The main thing to keep in mind is that consistency will give you the best chance to improve your skills regardless of your starting point. Hence, if you can devote a certain amount of time, on a regular basis, the likelihood of your Spanish skills improving will increase significantly.

So, please sit back and enjoy the short stories that have been prepared for you. They are designed to be both educational and entertaining. Please remember to go over them as many times as you need so that you can get the most out of the contents and materials presented in this book.

Let's move on to the next section in this book.

SECTION I:

The Verb "Essere/To Be" 22

Lesson 1: Present Simple with verb "essere" 23

Italiano	English
Il lavoro di tutti è importante	Everyone's Job Is Important
Vocabolario importante: Sindaco Ogni Città Scuola Successo funzionamento Insieme pazienti polizia Lavoro	Important vocabulary: Mayor every city school success functioning together patients police work
Il lavoro è importante nella mia città. Tutti i lavori sono importanti. I lavori della mia città	**Work** is very important in my **city**. All jobs are important. The jobs in mi city are:

sono: dottore, maestro, infermiera, commercialista, commesso, autista, ufficiale di polizia, cuoco, muratore, meccanico, elettricista e molti altri.

doctor, teacher, nurse, accountant, salesperson, driver, police officer, cook, builder, mechanic, electrician and many more.

I lavori delle persone nella mia città sono importanti affiché la città funzioni. I dottori sono necessari per i pazienti in ospedale. I pazienti vengono curati dai dottori. A scuola, un insegnante è essenziale per i bambini. I bambini sono felici con i bravi insegnanti.

The jobs that people do in my city are important for the **functioning** of the city. Doctors are necessary for patients in hospital. **Patients** are taken care of by doctors. At **school**, a teacher is essential for children. Children are happy with good teachers.

La città è sicura grazie alla polizia. Essi sono i responsabili della sicurezza di tutti. Gli autisti di autobus sono molto importanti. I meccanici, muratori ed elettricisti sono anch'essi molto importanti per la città. Ila loro lavoro è necessario per la sicurezza della città.

The city is safe because of the **police**. They are responsible for the safety of everyone. Bus drivers are very important. Mechanics, masons and electricians are also very important in the city. Their work is necessary for an efficient city.
The city mayor is the leader of the community.

Il sindaco della città è il leader della comunità. Il sindaco è incaricato del funzionamento della città. Senza il sindaco, il successo dei lavoratori non sarebbe possibile. Il sindaco è importante ma non è l'unico. Anche altre persone sono importanti. Per esempio, il capo della polizia è fondamentale. Senza il capo della polizia la sicurezza di una comunità è impossibile.

The **mayor** is in charge of running the city. Without the mayor, the **success** of all of the city's workers is not possible. The city mayor is important, but he is not the only one. Other people are important, too. For example, the chief of police is also a vital job for the community. With the chief of police, the security of the community is not possible.

Ogni persona è importante nella città. Io sono molto importante per la mia città. Sono un idraulico. Il mio lavoro è necessario in ogni casa nella mia città. Un buon idraulico è fondamentale in ogni città.

Every person is important in the city. Every person, with their job, is fundamental. I am very important to my community. I am a plumber. My job is necessary in every home in my city. A good plumber is vital to every community.

Anche i miei amici lo sono. Sono parte della comunità. con il loro lavoro sono parte della comunità. Sono bravi lavoratori. Insieme, siamo una comunità unita e ci dedichiamo al benessere di tutte le persone della nostra bellissima città.	My friends are also important to the city. They are a part of the community. With their work, they are a part of the community. They are good workers. **Together**, we are a united community and committed to the well-being of all of the people in our beautiful city.
E tu, qual è il tuo ruolo nella comunità?	And you, what is your job in your community?
Per favore rispondete alle seguenti domande.	Please answer the following questions.
Quali sono i lavori nella comunità? _____ _____ _____ _____	What are the jobs in the community? _____ _____ _____ _____
Chi è il responsabile del funzionamento della città? _____ _____ _____ _____	Who is responsible for running the city? _____ _____ _____
Chi è l'incaricato di dirigere la città? _____ _____ _____ _____	Who is in charge of the city's security? _____ _____ _____ _____
Quali sono i lavori più importanti in città? _____ _____ _____ _____	What are the most important jobs in the city? _____ _____ _____ _____
Chi sono le persone importanti in città? _____	Who are important people to the city? _____

_____ _____ _____	_____ _____ _____
Qual è il mio lavoro nella comunità?	What is my job in the community?
Perché i dottori sono importanti negli ospedali?	Why are doctors important in hospitals?
Perché i maestri sono fondamentali nelle scuole?	Why are teachers fundamental in schools?
Perché siamo tutti importanti nella città?	Why are we all vital in our community?
Quali sono i bravi lavoratori in città?	Who are good workers in the city?
Risposte suggerite	**Suggested answers**
Quali sono i lavori in città?	What are the jobs in the community?

Dottori, maestri, commessi, autisti sono lavori della comunità.	Doctors, teachers, salespeople, drivers are jobs in the community.
Chi è il responsabile del funzionamento della città?	Who is responsible for running the city?
Il sindaco è il responsabile del funzionamento della città.	The mayor is responsible of running the city.
Chi è l'incaricato della sicurezza della città?	Who is in charge of the city's security?
Il capo della polizia è l'incaricato della sicurezza della città.	The chief of police is in charge of the city's security.
Quali sono i lavori più importanti in città?	What are the most important jobs in the city?
Tutti i lavori sono importanti in città.	All jobs are important in the city.
Qual è il mio lavoro nella comunità?	What is my job in the community?
Sono un idraulico nella comunità.	I am a plumber in the community.
Perché i dottori sono importanti nelle città?	Why are doctors important in hospitals?
I dottori sono importanti per la salute dei pazienti.	Doctors are important for the care of patients.
Perché gli insegnanti sono importanti nelle scuole?	Why are teachers fundamental in schools?

I maestri sono fondamentali per la felicità dei bambini.	Teachers are fundamental for the happiness of children.
Perché siamo tutti fondamentali nella comunità?	Why are we all vital in our community?
Siamo tutti fondamentali perché i nostri lavori sono importanti.	We are all vital because our jobs are important.
Quali sono i bravi lavoratori in città?	Who are good workers in the city?
I miei amici sono bravi lavoratori in città.	My Friends are good workers in the city.

Lesson 2:
Present Simple with verb "essere" 30

Italiano	English
Una ragazza di nome Marcela	A Girl Named Marcela
Vocabolario importante:	Important vocabulary:
Appassionate	Fans
Scuola privata	Private school
Sportivo	Athlete
Eccitante	Exciting
Estroverse	Extroverted
Divertente	Handsome
Giovane	Young
Leghe	Leagues
D'aiuto	Helpful
Anche	Also
Ciao! Sono Marcela. Sono una ragazza giovane e amichevole. Sono anche molto attiva. Sono tante cose: alta, magra, logorroica, gentile, curiosa e un po' timida. Vengo da una città grande ed eccitante.	Hello! I am Marcela. I am a **young** and very friendly girl. I am also very active. I am many things: tall, thin, talkative, kind, curious and a bit shy. I am from a big and **exciting** city.
Anche le mie amiche sono molto attive. Sono appassionate di sport. Facciamo parte di una squadra di calcio e una di pallavolo. Anche le altre ragazze fanno parte del nostro team. Facciamo parte di due leghe sportive: una di calcio e una di pallavolo.	My friends are also very active. They are sports **fans**. We are part of two sports teams one soccer and one volleyball. Other girls are also part of our team. We are part of two sports **leagues**; one for soccer and one for volleyball.
Le mie migliori amiche sono Paola e Marta. Sono ragazze molto speciali. Siamo amiche, sorelle, compagne e socie. Sono estroverse, gentili, intelligenti e, soprattutto, creative. Per questo sono così popolari nella mia scuola. Definitivamente, sono le più popolari a scuola.	My best friends are Paola and Marta. They are very special girls. We are friends, sisters, classmates and partners. They are **extroverted**, kind, intelligent and, above all, creative. That is why they are so popular at my school. Definitely, they are the most popular at **school**. The boys are also kind and cheerful. They are not mean or aggressive. Quite the opposite,

Anche i ragazzi sono molto gentili e allegri. Non sono cattivi o aggressivi. Tutto il contrario, I ragazzi della mia scuola sono molto belli. Anche loro fanno parte delle squadre della scuola. Il mio amico Francesco è il più popolare a scuola. È un buon atleta e studente. Infatti, è il miglior studente della mia classe. È sempre il numero uno della classe.

I migliori amici di Luis e Guillermo. Sono molto divertenti. Sono alti e atletici. Sono anche dei buoni sportivi. Luis è un eccellente corridore. Guillermo fa boxe. È alto e forte, ma è anche molto gentile e umile. Sono dei bravi ragazzi.

Sono molto felice a scuola. Tutti i ragazzi della mia classe sono speciali. Sono tutti buoni amici. Non sono cattive persone. Al contrario, sono tutti molto gentili e d'aiuto. Siamo un buon gruppo di amici. Sono molto fortunata ad avere amici del genere a scuola.

Sono i migliori compagni in tutto l'universo!

the boys at my school are very nice. They are **also** part of the sports teams at my school. My friend Francisco is the most popular boy at school. He is a good **athlete** and student. In fact, he is the best student of my class. He is always number one in the class.

Francisco's best friends are Luis and Guillermo. They are very **handsome**. They are tall and athletic. They are also good athletes. Luis is an excellent runner. Guillermo is a boxer. He is tall and strong, but he is also very polite and humble. They are good boys.

I am very happy at my school. All of the kids in my class are special. They are all good friends. They are not bad people. Quite the opposite, they are all kind and **helpful** with me. We are a good group of friends. I am very lucky to have such good classmates at my school.

They are the best classmates in the entire universe!

Per favore rispondete alle seguente domande.   **Please answer the following questions.**

Com'è arcela?

What is Marcela like?

_____

_____

_____

_____

_____

_____

_____

_____

Com'è la città di Marcela?

What is Marcela's city like?

_____

_____

_____

_____

_____

_____

_____

_____

Come sono le amiche di Marcela?

What are Marcela's friends like?

_____

_____

_____

_____

_____

_____

_____

Di quali squadre fa parte Marcela?

_____

_____

_____

_____

What teams is Marcela a part of?

_____

_____

_____

_____

Com'è Francisco?

_____

_____

_____

_____

What is Francisco like?

_____

_____

_____

_____

Come sono gli amici di Francisco?

_____

_____

_____

_____

What are Francisco's friends like?

_____

_____

_____

_____

Qual è lo sport di Luis?

_____

_____

_____

_____

What is Luis' sport?

_____

_____

_____

_____

Qual è lo sport di Guillermo?   What is Guillermo's sport?

_____   _____

_____   _____

_____   _____

_____   _____

Come sono i ragazzi nella classe di Marcela?   What are the kids in Marcela's class like?

_____   _____

_____   _____

_____   _____

_____   _____

Perché è fortunata Marcela?   Why is Marcela lucky?

_____   _____

_____   _____

_____   _____

Risposte suggerite   Suggested answers

Com'è Marcela?   What is Marcela like?

Marcela è una ragazza giovane e amichevole.	Marcela is a young and very friendly girl.
Com'è la città di Marcela?	What is Marcela's city like?
La città di Marcela è molto grande ed emozionante.	Marcela's city is very big and exciting.
Come sono le amiche di Marcela?	What are Marcela's friends like?
Sono molto attive e appassionate di sport.	They are very active and fans of sports.
Di quali squadre fa parte Marcela?	What teams is Marcela a part of?
Marcela fa parte di una squadra di calcio e una di pallavolo.	Marcela is part of a soccer and a volleyball team.
Com'è Francisco?	What is Francisco like?
Francisco è un buon atleta e uno studente eccellente.	Francisco y a good athlete and an excellent student.
Come sono gli amici di Francisco?	¿Cómo son los amigos de Francisco?

Gli amici di Francesco sono divertenti, alti e atletici.

Francisco's friends are handsome, tall and athletic.

Qual è lo sport di Luis?

What is Luis' sport?

Luis è un corridore.

Luis is a runner.

Qual è lo sport di Guillermo?

What is Guillermo's sport?

Guillermo fa boxe.

Guillermo is a boxer.

Come sono i ragazzi della classe di Marcela?

What are the kids in Marcela's class like?

I ragazzi della classe di Marcela sono molto gentili e d'aiuto.

The kids in Marcela's class are very kind and helpful.

Perché Marcela è fortunata?

Why is Marcela lucky?

Marcela è fortunata perché ha i miglio compagni di tutto l'universo.

Marcela is lucky to have the best classmates in the universe.

Lesson 3:
Present Simple with verb "essere" 37

Italiano	English
Una vita sana	A Healthy Life

Vocabolario importante:	Important vocabulary:
attenzione	warning
amanti	lovers
bibide	drinks

Cibo spazzatura	junk food
consumo	consumption
disciplinato	disciplined
filosofia	philosophy
gusti	tastes
nutritivo	nutritious
Bevande gassate	soft drinks
sano	healthy

Il cibo sano è importante per una buona condizione fisica. Le persone sono sane con il cibo nutriente. Per esempio, verdure come: carote, patate, lattuga, pomodori e avocado sono molto ricchi e nutrienti. Frutta come: fragole, mele, pere, arance e banane sono anch'esse molto buone e nutrienti. Sono molto salutari per la famiglia e i preferite dei bambini.

Healthy food is necessary for good physical condition. People are healthy with **nutritious** food. For example, vegetables such as: carrots, potatoes, lettuce, tomatoes, and avocados are very rich and nutritious. Fruits like: strawberries, apples, pears, oranges and bananas are also delicious and nutritious. They are highly healthy for the whole family and children's favorites.

Sono felice del consumo di frutta e verdura. La salute è importante per una buona vita. Per me è molto importante il consumo di cibo che sia tanto delizioso quanto nutriente. Anche i miei amici amano il cibo sano e l'esercizio. Facciamo parte di una squadra dove tutti amano avere una vita sana.

I am enthusiastic about the **consumption** of fruits and vegetables. Health is important for a good life. For me, it is very important to consume food that is delicious but also full of vitamins. My friends are also fond of healthy food and exercise. We are members of an athletic club where we are all **lovers** of healthy life.

I miei fratelli non sono in forma. Amano il cibo spazzatura. Patatine, hamburger, pizza, pollo fritto e tacos sono i loro cibi preferiti. Le bevande gassate sono le loro bevande

My brothers are not healthy. They are addicted to **junk food**. French fries, hamburgers, pizza, fried chicken and tacos are their favorite foods. Soft drinks are their

preferite. Siamo molto diversi da questo punto di vista.

favorite **drinks**. We are very different in that sense.

Anche le mie cugine amano caffè, cioccolato, biscotti, torte e dolci. "Non siete in forma" è il mio avvertimento per loro. È difficile andarci a cena. Hanno gusti diversi dai miei. Ma siamo buone cugine e amiche.

My cousins are also addicted to coffee, chocolate, cookies, cakes and sweets. "You are not healthy," is my **warning** to them. It's hard to go out to dinner with them. They are of very different **tastes** than mine. But we are very good cousins and friends.

La mia filosofia è: se sei una persona sana, sei una persona felice. I miei amici la pensano allo stesso modo. Sono educati e si dedicano ad una vita sana. Anch'io sono educato. Sono felice con una vita sana.

My **philosophy** is: "if you are a healthy person, you are a happy person". My friends are of the same philosophy. They are disciplined and dedicated to healthy living. I am also **disciplined**. I am happy with a healthy life.

Il nuoto è il mio sport preferito. Il cibo sano è il mio preferito. Il cibo spazzatura è delizioso ma non è il mio preferito. Anche le bevande gassate son buoni ma non sono le mie preferite. Non amo il caffè ma è uno dei miei preferiti.

Swimming is my favorite sport. Healthy food is my favorite. Junk food is delicious, but it's not my favorite. **Soft drinks** are also very tasty, but they are not my favorite drinks. Water is my favorite drink. I am not addicted to coffee, but it is one of my favorite drinks.

E tu, qual è la tua dieta? E i tuoi cibi preferiti?

And you, what is your diet? What are your favorite foods?

Per favore rispondete alle seguenti domande.   Please answer the following questions.

Qual è il cibo necessario per una buona condizione fisica?

What food is necessary for a good physical condition?

_____   _____

_____   _____

_____   _____

_____

Come sono frutta e verdura?   How are fruits and vegetables?

_____

_____

_____   _____

_____   _____

_____

_____

Perché è importante la salute?   Why is health important?

_____   _____

_____   _____

_____   _____

_____   _____

Di quale squadra facciamo parte?

What club are we members of?

_____

_____

_____

_____

_____

_____

_____

_____

Cosa amano i miei fratelli?

What are my brothers addicted to?

_____

_____

_____

_____

_____

_____

_____

_____

Quali sono le bevande preferite dei miei fratelli?

What are my brothers' favorite drinks?

_____

_____

_____

_____

_____

_____

_____

_____

Qual è la mia filosofia?

What is my philosophy?

_____

_____

_____

_____

_____

_____

_____

_____

Perché son felice?	Why am I happy?

_____

_____

_____

_____

Qual è il mio sport preferito?	What is my favorite sport?

_____

_____

_____

_____

Qual è la mia bevanda preferita?	What is my favorite drink?

_____

_____

_____

_____

Risposte suggerite	Suggested answers

Qual è il cibo necessario per una buona condizione fisica?	What food is necessary for a good physical condition?

Il cibo sano è necessario per una buona vita.

Healthy food is necessary for a good life.

Como sono frutta e verdura?

How are fruits and vegetables?

Frutta e verdura sono molto buone e nutrienti.

Fruits and vegetables are very rich and nutritious.

Perché è importante la salute?

Why is health important?

La salute è importante per una buona vita.

Health is important for a good life.

Di quale squadra facciamo parte?

What club are we members of?

Facciamo parte di una squadra di atletica.

We are members of an athletic club.

Cosa amano i miei fratelli?

What are my brothers addicted to?

I miei fratelli amano il cibo spazzatura.

My brothers are addicted to junk food.

Quali sono le bevande preferite dei miei fratelli?

What are my brothers' favorite drinks?

Soft drinks are my brothers' favorite drinks

Le bevande gassate sono le preferite dei miei fratelli.

Qual è la mia filosofia?

What is my philosophy?

La mia filosofia è: se sei una persona sana, sei una persona felice.

My philosophy is: "if you are a healthy person, you are a happy person".

Perché sono felice?

Why am I happy?

Sono felice per la mia vita sana.

I am happy because of my healthy life.

Qual è il mio sport preferito?

What is my favorite sport?

Il nuoto è il mio sport preferito.

Swimming is my favorite sport.

Qual è la mia bevanda preferita?

What is my favorite drink?

L'acqua è la mia bevanda preferita.

Water is my favorite drink.

SECTION III:

The Present Simple Tense 94

Lesson 4:
Present Simple with "ARE" verbs

Italiano	English
Weekend al cinema	Weekend at the Cinema

Vocabolario importante:	Important vocabulary:
Biglietti	tickets
Conversazioni	conversations
Cinema	cinema
Uscite	releases

Weekend	weekend
Magnifico	great
Popcorn	popcorn
Passatempo	hobby
Film	movie
Sentimento	feeling

Il weekend è arrivato. È una buona opportunità per fare molte attività divertenti. Io e le mie amiche siamo emozionate per il nuovo film dei supereroi. È già al cinema. Compriamo sempre i biglietti per la premiere del film. Compro i biglietti davanti al cinema. È il luogo migliore per vedere il film.

The **weekend** is here. It is a good opportunity to do many fun activities. My friends and we are already excited for the new superhero movie. It is already in the cinema. We always buy the tickets for the premiere of the movie. I buy the tickets in front of the **cinema**. This is the best place to see the movie.

Solitamente spendiamo molti soldi sui biglietti migliori. Ma questo film è stupendo. Altre persone pagano meno per i biglietti ma i posti non sono i migliori. Regolarmente, compriamo popcorn, bevande gassate e caramelle. In realtà, non compriamo molto. Il mio amico Juan compra tanto popcorn.

We usually spend a lot of money on the best **tickets**. But this movie is amazing. Other people pay less for their tickets, but the seats are not good. Regularly, we buy **popcorn**, soft drinks and candy at the movies. Actually, we do not buy much. My friend Juan, he buys a lot of popcorn.

Amiamo il cinema. È il nostro passatempo nel weekend. Giochiamo anche a basket o nuotiamo nella piscina della città. Ma la nostra passione è il cinema. I miei amici amano i film d'azione. Anch'io amo i film

We love the cinema. It's our **hobby** on weekends. We also play basketball or swim in the pool of our community. But our passion is cinema. My friends love action

d'azione ma i miei preferiti sono i film d'amore. Mi piacciono molto le storie d'amore. Lasciano sempre una bella sensazione alla fine.

movies. I also love action movies. But my favorites are romance movies. I enjoy love stories very much. They always leave a nice **feeling** at the end.

Siamo pronti per l'inizio del film. Entrano più persone ma va bene perché il film non è ancora iniziato. Mi godo sempre i trailer prima dell'inizio del film. È bello sentitre di nuovi film. In questo modo siamo pronti per le nuove uscite.

Oh, il film sta per iniziare. Sembra geniale. Gli attori sono fantastici. Sono sicura che sia un ottimo film per iniziare il weekend. Finito il film, pranziamo a casa di Anna. I suoi piatti sono i migliori. Siamo tutti molto emozionati per le attività di questo weekend. È ovvio che sfruttiamo il fin settimana, no? La scuola non ci piace. Beh, non ci piacciono le lezioni di matematica ma ci piace parlare con gli amici. Gli amici sono la parte migliore della scuola.

We are ready for the beginning of the **movie**. More people enter, but it's okay because the movie has not started yet. I always enjoy the previews before the start of the film. It's good to hear about the new movies. Thus, we are ready for new **releases**.

Oh! The movie is about to start. It looks great. The actors are fantastic. I'm sure it's a great movie to start this weekend. After the movie, we have lunch at Ana's house. Her meals are the best. We are all very excited about the activities this weekend. It is clear that we enjoy the weekend, right? The school, we do not enjoy it. Well, we do not enjoy math classes, but we do have **conversations** with friends. Friends are the best part of school.

Rispondete per favore alle seguenti domande.

Please answer the following questions.

Perché siamo emozionati?

Why are we excited?

_____

_____

_____

_____

_____

_____

_____

_____

Cosa compriamo sempre?

What do we always buy?

_____

_____

_____

_____

_____

_____

_____

_____

Cos'è fantastico?

What is amazing?

_____

_____

_____

_____

_____

_____

_____

_____

Cosa compriamo solitamente al cinema?

What do we regularly buy at the cinema?

_____

_____

_____

_____

_____

_____

_____

_____

Qual è il nostro passatempo?

_____

_____

_____

_____

What is our hobby?

_____

_____

_____

_____

Quali film amano le mie amiche??

_____

_____

_____

_____

What movies do my friends love?

_____

_____

_____

_____

Cosa mi piace prima del film??

_____

_____

_____

_____

What do I enjoy before the movie?

_____

_____

_____

_____

Di cosa sono sicura?

_____

_____

_____

_____

What am I sure of?

_____

_____

_____

_____

Cosa facciamo dopo il film?

What do we do after the movie?

_____

_____

_____

_____

_____

_____

_____

_____

Cosa ci piace a scuola?

What do we enjoy at school?

_____

_____

_____

_____

_____

_____

_____

_____

Risposte suggerite

Suggested answers

Perché siamo emozionate?

Why are we excited?

Siamo emozionate per il weekend..

We are excited because it is the weekend.

Cosa compriamo sempre?

What do we always buy?

Compriamo sempre i migliori biglietti,

We always buy the best tickets.

Cos'è fantastico?

What is amazing?

Il nuovo film di supereroi è fantastico.

The new superhero film is amazing.

Cosa compriamo solitamente al cinema?

What do we regularly buy at the cinema?

Solitamente compriamo popcorn, sode e caramelle al cinema.

We regularly buy popcorn, sodas and candy at the cinema.

Qual è il nostro passatempo?

What is our hobby?

Il cinema è il nostro passatempo.

The cinema is our hobby.

Quali film amano le mie amiche?

What movies do my friends love?

Le mie amiche amano i film d'azione.

My Friends love action films.

Cosa mi piace prima del film?

What do I enjoy before the movie?

Mi piacciono i trailer prima del film.

I enjoy the previews before the movie.

Di cosa sono sicura?

What am I sure of?

Sono sicura che sia un ottimo film.

I am sure that it is a great movie.

Cosa facciamo dopo il film?

What do we do after the movie?

Pranziamo a casa di Ana.

We have lunch at Ana's house.

Cosa ci piace dopo la scuola?

What do we enjoy at school?

Ci piace parlare con gli amici.

We enjoy conversations among friends.

Lesson 5:
Present Simple with "ARE" verbs

Italiano	English
Viaggiare è un'esperienza magnifica	Traveling is a Wonderful Experience

Vocabolario importante:	Important vocabulary:
autentiche	authentic
desiderio	wish/want
esotici	exotic
affascinante	fascinating
fotografia	photograph/picture
meravigliosa	wonderful
natura	nature
provare	try
salutare	greet
tesoro	treasure

Viaggiare, non importa dove, è un'esperienza meravigliosa. Viaggiare è una di quelle attività che rendono la vita perfetta. Quando arrivi in un posto nuovo, l'esperienza di osservare i paesaggi, le persone, le case, le strade e la cultura è affascinante. Mi piace fare foto di tutto ciò che posso. Finisco sempre la pellicola per tutte le foto che faccio.

Traveling, anywhere, is a **wonderful** experience. Traveling is one of the activities that make life perfect. When you arrive at a new place, the experience of observing landscapes, people, houses, streets and culture is **fascinating**. I love taking pictures of everything I can. I always run out of memory in my camera because of all the pictures I take.

Voglio visitare posti esotici. Mi piace la giungla, la foresta, il mare e le avventure in posti emozionanti. C'è sempre qualcosa di nuovo da trovare in posti esotici. Mi piace molto visitare la natura.

I want to visit **exotic** places. I like the jungle, the forest, the sea and the adventures in exciting places. There is always something new to find in exotic places. I really like to visit **nature**.

Mi piace anche visitare luoghi storici. Per esempio le rovine, monumenti e luoghi famosi. Ogni città nel mondo è speciale. Vado sempre in strada. Cammino alla ricerca di nuovi tesori. Quando trovo un nuovo tesoro faccio subito una foto. Le foto sono il mio tesoro. Sono i ricordi di viaggi indimenticabili.

I also like to visit historical places. For example, I visit ruins, monuments and famous sites. Every city in the world is special. I always walk the streets. I walk ins search of new treasures. When I find a new **treasure**, I quickly take a picture of it. **Photographs** are my own treasures. They are the memories of unforgettable trips.

Ovunque, le persone ti salutano quando passi. Ti guardano e ti salutano. Mi piace parlare con la gente, beh, se parliamo la stessa lingua. Non sempre parliamo la stessa lingua ma comunichiamo sempre.

Everywhere, people **greet** when you pass. They look at you and greet you kindly. I like to chat with people, well, if we speak the same language. We do not always speak the same language, but we always communicate.

Anche il cibo è stupendo durante i viaggi Mi piacciono le specialità di ogni città o Paese. Le persone lavorano duramente per preparare dei cibi deliziosi. In tutti i Paesi vengono preparati piatti speciali. In molti posti il cibo è preparato per i turisti. Bevande tradizionali sono una parte importanti dell'esperienza locale. Mi piace provare bevande tradizionali ma non gli alcolici.

The food is also wonderful on every trip. I enjoy the **authentic** foods of each country or city. People work hard to prepare rich and delicious food. In all countries, something very special is cooked. In many places, special food is prepared for tourists. Traditional drinks are an important part of the local experience. I like to try traditional drinks, although I do not like alcoholic beverages.

47

Mi piace viaggiare. A parte il lavoro, è ciò che amo di più nella mia vita. Vorrei visitare tutti i Paesi del mondo. È qualcosa che voglio veramente fare. Una vita senza viaggi non è vita.

I love traveling. Aside from working, it's what I enjoy most in life. I **wish** to travel to all the countries of the world. This is something I really want to achieve. A life without traveling is not a life.

Per favore rispondete alle seguenti domande   Please answer the following questions.

Perché è affascinante arrivare in in posto   Why is it fascinating to arrive at a new place?
nuovo?

_____   _____

_____   _____

_____   _____

_____   _____

Quali posti voglio visitare?   What places do I want to visit?

_____   _____

_____   _____

_____   _____

_____   _____

Quali luoghi mi piacciono?   What places do I like?

_____   _____

_____   _____

_____   _____

_____   _____

Quali sono i luoghi storici che visito?   What are the historic places that I visit?

_____   _____

_____   _____

_____   _____

_____   _____

Cosa cerco quando cammino?

What do I search for when I walk?

_____

_____

_____

_____

_____

_____

_____

_____

Cosa fanno le persone quando passi?

What people do when people pass?

_____

_____

_____

_____

_____

_____

_____

_____

Com'è il cibo?

What is the food like?

_____

_____

_____

_____

_____

_____

_____

_____

Che cibo si prepara per i turisti?

What food is prepared for the tourists?

_____

_____

_____

_____

_____

_____

_____

_____

Quali bevande mi piace provare?

What drinks do I like to try?

_____

_____

_____

_____

_____

_____

_____

_____

Cosa vorrei fare?

What do I wish to do?

_____

_____

_____

_____

_____

_____

_____

_____

Risposte suggerite

Suggested answers

Perché è affascinante arrivare in posti nuovi?

Why is it fascinating to arrive at a new place?

È affascinante arrivare in posti nuovi perché puoi osservare paesaggi, persone, case e strade.

It is fascinating to arrive at a new place because you can observe landscapes, people, houses and streets.

Che luoghi voglio visitare?

What places do I want to visit?

Voglio visitare luoghi esotici come giungle e foreste.

I want to visit exotics places such as jungles and forests

Quale luogo mi piace?

What place do I like?

Mi piace molto la natura.

I like nature very much.

Quali sono i luoghi storici che visito?

What are the historic places that I visit?

Visito luoghi storici come rovine e monumenti.

I visit historic places such as ruins and monuments

Cosa cerco quando cammino?

What do I search for when I walk?

I search for treasures when I walk on the streets.

Cerco tesori quando cammino per le strade.

Che fanno le persone quando passi?

What people do when you pass?

Le persone ti salutano quando passi.

People greet you when you pass.

Com'è il cibo?

What is the food like?

Il cibo è ricco e delizioso.

The food is rich and delicious.

Quale cibo si prepara ai turisti?

What food is prepared for the tourists?

Si preparano cibi autentici per i turisti.

They prepare authentic food for tourists.

Quali bevande mi piace provare?

What drinks do I like to try?

Mi piace provare bibite tradizionali.

I like to try traditional drinks.

Cosa voglio fare?

What do I wish to do?

Voglio visitare tutti i Paesi del mondo.

I wish to visit all of the countries in the world.

Lesson 6:
Present Simple with "ARE" verbs

Italiano	English
I soldi	Money

Vocabolario importante:	Important vocabulary:
Risparmiare	save
Apprezzare	appreciate
Sforzo	effort
Facile	easy
Aiuta	helps
Spese	expenses
Dimenticare	forget
Pagare	pay
Saldo	salary

Vite

lives

Il denaro è una parte importante delle nostre vite. In particolare, le nostre vite dipendono dai soldi che guadagniamo. Più guadagniamo, più la nostra vita è facile. Se non guadagniamo tanti soldi allora la nostra vita diventa un po' più difficile.

Money is an important part of all our lives. In particular, our **lives** depend on the money we earn. If we earn a lot of money, our life is a little easier. If we do not earn a lot of money, then our life is a bit more difficult.

Guadagnare denaro non è facile. Tutti vogliono guadagnare soldi. Dopotutto, chi non vuole guadagnare soldi senza lavorare? Però non è facile guadagnare senza lavorare. Guadagnare soldi richiede uno sforzo. Ovviamente la vita non è solo guadagnare soldi. È vero, i soldi sono necessari per pagare ciò che vogliamo. Dobbiamo pagare la casa, le spede giornaliere, il cibo e i vestiti. Tutto questo è importante. Ma le persone che pensno soltanto ai soldi non sono felici.

Making money is not **easy**. Everyone wants easy money. After all, who does not like to earn a lot of money without working? But, it is not easy to make money without working. It always takes an **effort** to earn money.

Of course, life is not just about making money. It is true, money is necessary to **pay** for the things we need. We need to pay for our house, the daily **expenses**, the food and the clothes we use. All this is important in life. But people who only think about money are not totally happy.

I soldi sono un mezzo per godere della vita. Le persone e le esperienze sono le cose più essenziali nella vita. Se apprezzi le persone nella tua vita, sarai sempre felice. Non dimenticare che la vita vale più dei soldi.

Money is used as a means to enjoy life. People and experiences are the most essential things in life. If you **appreciate** the people in your life, you are always happy. Do not **forget** that life is more than money.

"Non spendere tutti i tuoi soldi. Risparmia sempre."

"Do not spend all your money. Always keep a little "

Queste sono le parole di mio nonno. Crede che spendere tutti i soldi non sia una buona idea. Che è vero. È importante risparmiare. Mi preparo sempre al futuro. Non spendo tutti i miei soldi. Tra l'altro, risparmiare mi permette di aiutare la mia famiglia.

Those are the words of my grandfather. He believes that spending all your money is not a good idea. That is very true. It is necessary to **save** a part. I always prepare for the future. I do not spend all my money. Also, saving money **helps** me to help my family.

Grazie al mio lavoro guadagno bene. Non sono un milionario ma il mio stipendio è buono. Guadagno abbastanza da pagare le varie spese e risparmiare un po' per la fine del mese. I miei risparmi mi permettono di andare in vacanza e di comprare una nuova macchina. In breve, i soldi sono importanti ma non sono la cosa più importante nella vita. Ricordati di godere della vita. Non fissarti sui soldi.

Due to my job, I earn well. I'm not a millionaire, but my **salary** is good. I earn enough to pay all my expenses and save a little at the end of the month. My savings help me take vacations and buy me a new car. In short, money is important, but it is not the most important thing in life. Remember to enjoy life. Do not get obsessed with money.

Per favore rispondete alle seguenti domande.

Please answer the following questions.

Perché i soldi non sono importanti nelle nostre vite?

Why is money important in our lives?

_____

_____

_____

_____

_____

_____

_____

Che succede quando facciamo tanti soldi?

What happens if we make a lot of money?

_____

_____

_____

_____

_____

_____

Che succede se facciamo pochi soldi?

_____

_____

_____

_____

What happens if we make a little money?

_____

_____

_____

_____

Perché i soldi sono necessari?

_____

_____

_____

_____

Why is money necessary?

_____

_____

_____

_____

A cosaserve il denaro?

_____

_____

_____

_____

What is money used for?

_____

_____

_____

_____

Quali sono le parole di mio nonno?

_____

_____

_____

_____

What are my grandfather's words?

_____

_____

_____

_____

Cosa permettono di fare i soldi?

What does money help to do?

_____

_____

_____

_____

_____

_____

_____

_____

Perché il mio salario è buono?

Why is my salary good?

_____

_____

_____

_____

_____

_____

_____

_____

A cosa serve il mio stipendio?

What is the money in my salary for?

_____

_____

_____

_____

_____

_____

_____

_____

Cosa devi ricordare?

What must you remember?

_____

_____

_____

_____

_____

_____

_____

_____

Risposte suggerite

Suggested answers

Perché i soldi sono importanti nella nostra vita?

Why is money important in our lives?

I soldi sono importanti perché le nostre vite dipendono da essi.

Money is important because our lives depend on it.

Che succede se facciamo tanti soldi?

What happens if we make a lot of money?

La vita è leggermente più facile.

It makes life a little easier.

Che succede se facciamo pochi soldi?

What happens if we make a little money?

La vita è leggermente più difficile.

It makes life a little harder.

Perché i soldi sono necessari?

Why is money necessary?

I soldi sono necessari per pagare tutto ciò di cui abbiamo bisogno.

Money is necessary to pay for all the things we need.

Per cosa si usano i soldi?	What is money used for?
I soldi sono un mezzo per godersi la vita.	Money is used as a means of enjoying life.
Quali sono le parole di mio nonno?	What are my grandfather's words?
Non spende tutti i tuoi soldi. Risparmia sempre.	Don't spend all of your money. Always save a little.
Cosa ti permettono di fare i soldi??	What does money help to do?
Risparmiare mi permette di aiutare la mia famiglia.	Saving money helps me support my family.
Perché è buono il mio stipendio?	Why is my salary good?
Perché posso pagare le spese e risparmiare alla fine del mese.	Because I can pay for all of my expenses and save a little at the end of the month.
A cosa serve il mio stipendio?	What is the money in my salary for?

Il mio salario serve per andare in vacanza e comprare una nuova auto.

The money from my salary serves to go on vacation and buy a new car.

Cosa devi ricordarti?

What must you remember?

Non fissarti sul denaro.

Don't become obsessed with money.

SECTION IV:

The Present Continuous Tense

Lesson 7:
Present Continuous Tense

Italiano	English
Cambi nella società	Changes in society

Vocabolario importante:	Important vocabulary:
Boschi	forests
Vero	true
Criticare	criticizing
Investire	investing
Lontano	faraway
Principi	principles
Progetto	project

Società	society
Tecnologia	technology
Violenza	violence

La società sta cambiando. Ogni giorno c'è una nuova invenzione o una nuova idea. Musica, moda e tecnologia cambiano giornalmente. Questo perché anche il modo di pensare delle persone sta cambiando. Adesso, molti usano la tecnologia in maniera produttiva. Ci sono molte persone che colgono l'occasione di migliorare attraverso questi cambi.

Society is changing. Every day there is a new invention or a new idea. Music, fashion and technology change daily. That is why the way of thinking for many people is also changing. Now, many are using **technology** in a productive way. There are many people who are taking advantage of changes in society for the better.

Al momento, le opportunità di crescita stanno aumentando. Queste opportunità ti permettono di imparare cose nuove, conoscere posti diversi o comunicare con persone di luoghi lontani. I Paesi investono molto sullo sviluppo di importanti infrastrutture. Per esempio, molti Paesi stanno migliorando i loro network.

Currently, growth opportunities are increasing. These opportunities allow you to learn new things, to know different places or to communicate with other people in **faraway** places. Countries are **investing** a lot in developing important infrastructure. For example, many countries are growing their internet network.

Ma ci sono persone che criticano i cambi nella società. Queste persone dicono che la società sta perdendo i suoi principi e valori. Questi cambi non portano risultati positivi. Al contrario, fanno del male ai giovani.

But, there are people who are **criticizing** the changes in society. These people say that society is losing its **principles** and values. The changes are not providing positive things. On the contrary, they are hurting young people.

Ciò che è certo è che ci sono sia cose buone che cattive. Ma credo che stia tutto migliorando. Nella mia città, facciamo il meglio per migliorare la situazione. Vogliamo ridurre la violenza, migliorare le scuole e migliorare la salute. È un compito difficile ma insieme possiamo farcela. E soprattutto le autorità supportano le nostre iniziative per migliorare le condizioni di vita della città.

It is **true** that there are always good and bad things. But I think things are improving. In my city, we are doing our best to improve the situation. We want to reduce **violence**, increase schools, and improve health. It is a hard task, but together we are achieving them. Mainly, the authorities of our city are supporting the initiatives that we have to improve the living conditions in the city.

Il progetto più importante è la raccolta della spazzatura. Incoraggiamo le persone a non buttare la spazzatura in strada. Facciamo il nostro meglio per ridurre l'ammontare di spazzatura nelle strade e in acqua. Conserviamo anche l'acqua e proteggiamo le foreste. Penso che abbiamo una buona opportunità per fare dei cambi positivi nella città. Siamo tutti ottimisti. Insieme possiamo farcela. Abbiamo ancora del lavoro da fare ma stiamo facendo il nostro dovere nella comunità.

The most important **project** that we are promoting is garbage collection. We are encouraging people not to throw garbage on the street. We are doing our best to reduce the amount of garbage on the streets and in the water. We are also conserving water and protecting **forests**. I think we have a good opportunity to make very positive changes in our city. We are all being optimists. Together we are achieving it. We still have work to do, but we are fulfilling our duty with our community.

Per favore rispondete alle seguenti domande.   Please answer the following questions.

Cosa sta cambiando?   What is changing?

_____   _____

_____   _____

_____   _____

_____   _____

Cosa molti usano in maniera produttiva?   What are many using in a productive manner?

_____   _____

_____   _____

_____   _____

_____   _____

Cosa sta aumentando al momento?   What is currently increasing?

_____   _____

_____   _____

_____   _____

_____   _____

In cosa investono i Paesi?

_____

_____

_____

_____

What are countries investing in?

_____

_____

_____

_____

Cosa è certo?

_____

_____

_____

_____

What is true?

_____

_____

_____

_____

Cosa vogliamo ridurre?

_____

_____

_____

_____

What do we want to reduce?

_____

_____

_____

_____

Qual è il progetto più importante al momento?

_____

_____

_____

_____

What is the most important project that we are currently promoting?

_____

_____

_____

_____

Cosa stiamo conservando?

What are we currently conserving?

_____

_____

_____

_____

_____

_____

_____

_____

Risposte suggerite

Suggested answers

Cosa sta cambiando?

What is changing?

La società sta cambiando

Society is changing.

Cosa molti usano in maniera produttiva?

What are many using in a productive manner?

Molti usano la tecnologia in maniera produttiva.

Many are using technology in a productive manner.

Cosa sta aumentando al momento?

What is currently increasing?

<u>Le opportunità di crescita stanno aumentando.</u>	<u>Growth opportunities are currently increasing.</u>
In cosa investono i Paesi?	What are countries investing in?
<u>I Paesi investono nelle infrastrutture.</u>	
	<u>Countries are investing in infrastructure.</u>
Cosa è certo?	What is true?
<u>È certo che ci sono sia cose buone che cattive.</u>	<u>It is true that there are good things and bad things.</u>
Cosa vogliamo ridurre?	What do we want to reduce?
<u>Vogliamo ridurre la violenza.</u>	<u>We want to reduce violence.</u>
Qual è il progetto più importante?	What is the most important project that we are promoting?

Il progetto più importante è la raccolta della spazzatura.

The most important project that we are promoting is garbage collection.

Cosa stiamo conservando?

What are we conserving?

Stiamo conservando l'acqua e stiamo prroteggendo le foreste.

We are conserving water and protecting the forests.

SECTION V:

The Present Simple: Irregular Verbs

Lesson 8:
Present Simple Tense: Irregular Verbs

Italiano	English
Il mio sogno è viaggiare	My Dream is to Travel

Vocabolario importante:	Important vocabulary:
In giro	around
Dire	tell
Fantastico	lovely
Incredibile	incredible
Laghi	lakes
Montagne	mountains
Prospettive	perspective
Spiagge	beaches

Mi piacerebbe viaggiare in tutto il mondo. Conosco molto posti. Conosco Parigi, Londra e Amsterdam. Sono città bellissime. Ci soo molte cose speciali. C'è sempre qualcosa di nuovo da vedere. Conosco anche

I like to travel around the world. I know many places. I know Paris, London and Amsterdam. They are very beautiful cities. They have many special things. There is always something new to see. I also know

l'Africa. Il mio Paese preferito è il Sud Africa. È un Paese così bello ed esotico.

Africa. My favorite place is South Africa. It is such a beautiful and exotic country.

Pero ci sono anche molti posti che non conosco. Ad esempio, non so molto sul Sud America. Mi piacerebbe esplorare il Brasile o la Colombia. Il mio migliore amico è stato in Brasile. Lui e la sua famiglia conoscono molti posti in Brasile. Mi han detto che è un Paese fantastico. Ha anche delle incredibili spiagge.

But there are many places that I do not know. For example, I do not know South America. I would like to know Brazil or Colombia. My best friend knows Brazil. He and his family know many places in Brazil. They tell me it's a lovely country. It also has incredible beaches.

Un altro posto che non conosco è il Canada. È un Paese così grande e pieno di storia. Un mio collega conosce Montreal. Mi ha detto che è una città bellissima e piena di cultura. Devo assolutamente vedere Montreal!

Another place I do not know is Canada. It is such a big country and full of history. A co-worker knows Montreal. He tells me that it is a beautiful city and full of cultural life. I must know Montreal!

Io e la mia famiglia conosciamo molti posti nel mondo. Ma ci sono molti posti che non conosciamo nel nostro di Paese. Siamo appassionati di siti storici e città magiche. C'è ancora tanto da vedere.

My family and I know many places in our country. We know **beaches, mountains** and **lakes**. But there are still many places that we do not know in our country. We are very keen to know some historical sites and magical towns. There is still much to know.

E tu, che posti conosci? Se conosci molti posti allora sei fortunato. Sei fortunato a conoscere molti posti. Se non ne conosci molti, dovresti viaggiare di più. Le persone che conoscono molti posti hanno una prospettiva diversa della vita. Queste sono persone molto interessanti. Hanno molte storie da raccontare.

And you, what places do you know? If you know many places, you are lucky. You are lucky to know many places. If you do not know many places, you should travel more. People who know many different places are people with a different **perspective** of the world. These people are more interesting. They have many stories to **tell**.

Credo ci sia sempre qualcosa da scoprire. Sono sicuro di non conoscere tutti luoghi magnifici del pianeta. Ci sono così tanti posti incredibili in tutti i Paesi del mondo.

I think there is always a new place to know. I'm sure I do not know all the wonderful places in the world. That is why I want to travel. There are so many **incredible** places in every country in the world.

Oh, purtroppo ho pochi soldi. Devo lavorare di più. Conosco molti modi per guadagnare dei soldi in più. Quindi, lavorare per risparmiare e viaggiare. Solo allora potrò visitare tutti i luoghi speciali nel mio Paese e in giro per il mondo.

h, but I do not have much money! I need to work more. I know many ways to earn extra money. So, I work to save a little money and travel. Only then can I know the most special places in my country and **around** the world.

Per favore rispondete alle seguenti domande.   Please answer the following questions.

Quali città conosco?   What cities do I know?

_____   _____

_____   _____

_____   _____

_____   _____

Qual è il mio posto preferito in Africa?   What is my favorite place in Africa?

_____   _____

_____   _____

_____   _____

_____   _____

Quali posti non conosco?   What place do I not know?

_____   _____

_____   _____

_____   _____

_____   _____

Com'è il Brasile?   What is Brazil like?

_____   _____

_____   _____

_____   _____

_____   _____

Com'è Montreal?

_____

_____

_____

_____

What is Montreal like?

_____

_____

_____

_____

Quali luoghi conosciamo come famiglia?

_____

_____

_____

_____

What places do we know as a family?

_____

_____

_____

_____

Cosa devi fare se non conosci molti posti?

_____

_____

_____

_____

What must you do if you don't know too many places?

_____

_____

_____

Cosa penso?

_____

_____

_____

_____

What do I think?

_____

_____

_____

_____

Risposte suggerite

Suggested answers

Che città conosco?

What cities do I know?

Conosco Parigi, Londra e Amsterdam.

I know Paris, London and Amsterdam.

Qual è il mio posto preferito in Africa?

What is my favorite place in Africa?

Il mio posto preferito in Africa è il Sud Africa.

My favorite place in Africa is South Africa.

Quali luoghi non conosco?

What place do I not know?

Non conosco il Sud America.

I don't know South America.

Com'è il Brasile?

What is Brazil like?

Mi dicono che è un Paese fantastico.

I hear that Brazil is a lovely country.

Com'è Montreal?

What is Montreal like?

È una città bellissima e piena di cultura.	It is a beautiful city and filled with lots of cultural life.
¿Quali posti conosciamo come famiglia?	What places do we know as a family?
Conosciamo spiagge, montagne e laghi.	We know beaches, mountains, and lakes.
Cosa devi fare se non conosci molti posti?	What must you do if you don't know too many places?
Se non conosci molti posti devi viaggiare di più.	If you don't know many places, then you must travel more.
Cosa penso?	What do I think?
Penso ci sia sempre qualche posto da scoprire.	I think there is always a new place to know.

Lesson 9:
Present Simple Tense: Irregular Verbs

Italiano	English
Egoista o generoso	Selfish or Generous

Vocabolario importante:	Important vocabulary:
Costruttivo	constructive
Distruttivo	destructive
Egoista	selfish
Generosa	generous
Opposto	opposite
Sicurezza	security
Loro stesse	themselves
Laboriose	hardworking

"Voglio questo" o "Voglio quello" sono frasi comuni di persone egoiste, e ciò significa che non pensano ad altro che a loro stesse. Queste persone vogliono tutto per loro. Non si interessano degli altri. Vogliono tutto per se stesse.

"I want this," or "I want the other" are common phrases of **selfish** people, that is, people who do not think of anyone but **themselves**. These people only want things for themselves. They do not care for anyone else. They want everything for themselves.

Questo è un atteggiamento distruttivo. Quando una persona è egoista questa non vuole il meglio per gli altri. Vogliono il meglio solo per loro stessi. Questo atteggiamento è distruttivo perché influenzano le persone in maniera negativa.

This is a **destructive** attitude. When a person is very selfish, they do not want the best for others. They only want the best for themselves. This attitude is destructive because it affects other people in a negative way.

L'opposto di una persona egoista è una persona generosa. Questo genere di persona vuole sempre il meglio per gli altri. Una persona generosa vuole aiutare gli altri. Sono persone con un atteggiamento costruttivo.

The **opposite** of a selfish person is a **generous** person. This type of person always wants the best for others. A generous person always wants to help others. They are people with a **constructive** attitude.

We want the best for you

Noi vogliamo il meglio per te.

I remember that phrase from my parents. They are generous people. They always want the best for us. Now that we are older, we understand why our parents always want the best for us.

Ricordo questa frase dei miei genitori. Sono persone generose. Vogliono sempre il meglio per noi. Adesso che siamo grandi, capiamo perché i nostri genitori volessero sempre il meglio   per   noi.

Voglio il meglio per me stesso e per gli altri.
Voglio anche il meglio per la mia città. Tutti
vogliamo lo stesso nell nostra città.
Vogliamo sicurezza e tranquillità. Vogliamo
vivere in una città ideale per le nostre
famiglie.

I want the best for myself and for others. I
also want the best for my community. We all
want the same in our community. We want
security and tranquility. We want to live in
an ideal place for our families.

Nella nostra comunità non vogliamo
persone negative. Non vogliamo persone
egoiste. Nella nostra città vogliamo persone
ottimiste. Vogliamo persone laboriose.
Siamo sicuri di volere tutti la stessa cosa in
città.

In our community, we do not want people
with bad attitudes. We do not want selfish
people. In our community we want
optimistic people. We want **hardworking**
people. We are sure that we want the same
for our community.

E tu, cosa vuoi nella tua comunità? Se tutti
vogliono la stessa cosa è facile lavorare come
squadra. Se non volete tutti la stessa cosa
allora è difficile lavorare come squadra.

And you, what do you want in your
community? If everyone wants the same, it is
easy to work as a team. Now, if you do not
want the same, then it is more difficult to
work as a team.

We want an united and optimistic
community.

Vogliamo una comunità unita e ottimista.

È la filosofia delle persone che vivono in
questa città. Se vuoi una città unita, è
importante lavorare in squadra con gli stessi
obiettivi.

That is the philosophy of the people who live
in this community. If you want a united
community, it is important to work as a team
with common goals and objectives.

Per favore rispondete alle seguenti domande.   Please answer the following questions.

Quali sono le frasi comuni di persone egoiste?   What are the common phrases of selfish people?

_____   _____

_____   _____

_____   _____

_____   _____

Cosa vogliono le persone egoiste?   What do selfish people want?

_____   _____

_____   _____

_____   _____

_____   _____

Perché questo è un atteggiamento negativo?   Why is this a destructive attitude?

_____   _____

_____   _____

_____   _____

_____   _____

Qual è l'opposto di una persona egoista?   What is the opposite of a selfish person?

_____   _____

_____   _____

_____   _____

Quali sono le parole dei miei genitori?

What is my parents' phrase?

_____

_____

_____

_____

_____

_____

_____

_____

Cosa voglio per gli altri?

What do I want for others?

_____

_____

_____

_____

_____

_____

_____

_____

Cosa vogliamo per la nostra comunità?

What do we want in our community?

_____

_____

_____

_____

_____

_____

_____

_____

Quali persone vogliamo nella nostra comunità?

What people do we want in our community?

_____

_____

_____

_____

_____

_____

_____

_____

Risposte suggerite	Suggested answers
Quali sono le frasi comuni delle persone egoiste?	What are the common phrases of selfish people?
"Voglio questo" o "Voglio quello" sono frasi comuni delle persone egoiste.	"I want this" or "I want the other" are the common phrases of selfish people.
Cosa vogliono le persone egoiste?	What do selfish people want?
Vogliono tutto per loro stesse.	They want everything for themselves.
Perché questo è un atteggiamento distruttivo?	Why is this a destructive attitude?
Questo atteggiamento è distruttivo perché influenza gli altri in maniera negativa.	This attitude is destructive because it affects other people in a negative manner.
Qual è l'opposto di una persona egoista?	What is the opposite of a selfish person?
L'opposto di una persona egoista è una persona generosa.	The opposite of a selfish person is a generous person.

Quali sono le parole dei miei genitori?

What is my parents' phrase?

Vogliamo il meglio per voi.

We want the best for you.

Cosa voglio per gli altri?

What do I want for others?

Voglio anch'io il meglio per gli altri.

I also want the best for others.

Cosa vogliamo nella nostra comunità?

What do we want in our community?

Vogliamo pace e tranquillità nella nostra comunità.

We want peace and tranquility in our community

Che persone vogliamo nella nostra comunità?

What people do we want in our community?

We want optimistic and hardworking people.

Vogliamo persone ottimiste e laboriose.

Lesson 10:
Present Simple Tense: Irregular Verbs

Italiano	English
Il negozio è chiuso	The Store is Closed

Vocabolario importante:	Important vocabulary:
Qualcuno	anyone/someone
Correre	rushing
Isolati	blocks
Giornale	newspaper
Insolito	unusual
Letto	milk
Mistero	mystery
Fretta	hurry
Velocemente	quickly
Andiamo	let's go

Dove va il signor Lopez?	Where is Mr. López going?
Qualcuno lo sa?	Does **anyone** know?
No?	No?

Il signor Lopez va al negozio vicino casa sua per comprare il latte ogni mattina. Esce di casa, cammina per sei isolati, compra il latte e torna a casa. Ma oggi va in un altro posto. Non sta andando al negozio. Cammina velocemente.

Mr. López goes to the store near his house to buy **milk** every morning. He leaves his house, walks six **blocks**, buys the milk and returns to his house. But today it goes to another place. He is not going to the store. He is walking **quickly**.

Dove sta andando?

Where is he going?

Oggi è un giorno normale. È un giorno come un altro. C'è il sole e fa caldo. I bambini stanno correndo a scuola perché sono in ritardo. Molte persone corrono per arrivare a lavoro in orario.

Today is a normal day. It's a day like any other. It's sunny and it's a bit warm. The children are running to school because they're a little late. Many people are also **rushing** to get to work on time.

But, Mr. López is walking in a hurry. He only passes by, greeting people he meets, but he does not talk to them as he usually does. Today, he has some important activity to do.

Ma il signor Lopez va di fretta. Saluta le persone che incontra ma non parla con loro come fa sempre. Oggi, ha delle faccendei mportanti da sbrigare.

Andiamo a prendere il latte

- **Let's go** for milk

Gli dice il suo amico, il signor Pérez.

His friend, Mr. Pérez, tells him.

85

Pero il signor Lopez continua a camminare. È molto strano. Il signor López compra il latte da anni in quel negozio. In più, compra il giornale e il pane. È la sua dayly routine. Ma oggi è diverso. Oggi c'è qualcosa di diverso. Oggi sta succedendo qualcosa.

But Mr. López just keeps going. This is **unusual**. Mr. López has been buying his milk at the local store years every day for many. In addition, he buys the **newspaper** and fresh bread. This is his daily routine. But today it is not like that. Today, there is something different. Something is happening.

Sta succedendo qualcosa di strano: il signor López entra in un altro negozio.

Perché sta entrando in un altro negozio?

Oh! Il mistero è risolto. Il negozio dove va solitamente il signor López è chiuso! Ecco perché va in un altro negozio. Per questo va di fretta. L'altro negozio è più lontano da casa. È lontano nove isolati. Devi camminare molto per arrivarci.

Something unusual is happening: Mr. López enters another store.

Why is he entering another store?

Oh! The **mystery** is solved. The shop where Mr. López usually goes is closed! That's why he goes to another store. That's why he's in such a **hurry**. The other store is farther from his house. It's nine blocks from his house. You must walk a lot to get to the other store.

Adesso il signor López ha il latte fresco. Sta andando al panificio. Compra il giornale come sempre. Tutto è tornato alla normalità.

Now, Mr. López brings his fresh milk. He is going to the bakery for fresh bread. He is buying his newspaper as usual. Everything is back to normal.

Perché il solito negozio è chiuso? È un mistero.

Why is the regular store closed? That is a mystery.

Per favore rispondete alle seguenti domande.   Please answer the following questions.

Dove compra il latte il signor López?   Where does Mr. López buy milk?

_____

_____

_____

_____

Per quanti isolati cammina?   How many blocks does he walk?

_____

_____

_____

_____

Perché le persone stanno correndo?   Why are many people rushing?

_____

_____

_____

_____

Perché il signor López non parla con le persone che saluta come fa sempre?   Why doesn't he talk with the people that greet Mr. López like he always does?

_____

_____

_____

_____

Qual è la routine giornaliera del signor López?

_____

_____

_____

_____

What is Mr. López's everyday routine?

_____

_____

_____

_____

Cosa è insolito?

_____

_____

_____

What is unusual?

_____

_____

_____

Cosa succede con il solito negozio?

_____

_____

_____

_____

What's happening with the usual store?

_____

_____

_____

_____

Perché il solito negozio è chiuso?

_____

_____

_____

_____

Why is the usual store closed?

_____

_____

_____

_____

Risposte suggerite	Suggested answers
Dove va il signor López a comprare il latte?	Where does Mr. López buy milk?
Il signor López va a comprare il latte in un negozio vicino casa.	Mr. López goes to buy milk a store near his home.
Per quanti isolati cammina?	How many blocks does he walk?
Cammina per sei isolati.	He walks six blocks.
Perché molte persone corrono?	Why are many people rushing?
Corrono per arrivare a lavoro in tempo.	They are rushing to get to work on time.
Perché il signor López non parla con le persone che saluta come fa sempre?	Why doesn't he talk with the people that greet Mr. López like he always does?
Perché il signor López va di fretta.	Because Mr. López is walking in a hurry.

Qual è la routine giornaliera del signor López?	What is Mr. López's everyday routine?
Compra il latte, il pane e il giornale.	He buys milk, fresh bread and the newspaper.
Cos'è insolito?	What is unusual?
Il signor López entra in un altro negozio.	Mr. López enters another store.
Cosa succede con il solito negozio?	What's happening with the usual store?
Il solito negozio è chiuso	The usual store is closed.
Perché il solito negozio è chiuso?	Why is the usual store closed?
È un mistero.	It is a mystery.

SECTION VI:

Bringing It All Together

Lesson 11:
Bringing it all together

Italiano	English
Natale	Christmas

Vocabolario importante:	Important vocabulary:
Attivamente	actively
Anziani	elderly
Cristiana	Christian
Epoca	time
Necessità	needy
Divertirsi	have a good time
Pace	peace
Poveri	poor

Religioso	religious
Volontari	volunteer

Il natale è celebrato in molti Paesi in giro per il mondo. Questa festa è prevalentemente cristiana. Il natale è la celebrazione del compleanno di Gesù Cristo. Pertanto ci sono molti costumi legati alla religione cristiana.

Christmas is celebrated in many countries around the world. This celebration is mainly of **religious** origin. Christmas is the celebration of the birth of Jesus Christ. Therefore, there are many customs related to the **Christian** religion.

Ma il natale è anche una festa di famiglia. Il natale è un'occasione dove molte famiglie si riuniscono pur vivendo in Paesi o continenti diversi. Il natale è un'opportunità per dimenticare i propri problemi e divertirsi con famiglia e amici.

But Christmas is also a family celebration. Christmas is an occasion where many families gather despite living in different countries or even continents. Christmas is an opportunity to forget about problems and **have a good time** together with family and friends.

Un'altra caratteristica importante del natale è la generosità. Durante il periodo viene fatta tanta carità. Molte persone danno soldi alle associazioni come la Salvation Army. Queste organizzazioni fanno sempre il meglio per le persone bisognose. Altre organizzazioni aiutano i bambini e gli anziani. L'importante è aiutare chi ne ha bisogno.

Another important characteristic of Christmas is generosity. In this age, charity is practiced. Many people give money to charities like the Salvation Army. These organizations are always doing positive things for **poor** and **needy** people. Other organizations are involved with children and the **elderly**. The important thing is to help the people who need it.

Forse il miglior lato del natale è quello commerciale. In questo periodo, molti negozi hanno offerte speciali su vestiti, roba elettronica, giocattoli e altri oggetti. Dato che il natale è un periodo per dare cose bellissime a famiglia e amici, il consumismo non dovrebbe essere l'unica ragione per celebrarlo.

Perhaps the best-known aspect is the commercial side of Christmas. During this time, many businesses have special offers on clothing, electronics, toys and many other items. While Christmas is a **time** to give beautiful things to family and friends, consumerism should not be the only reason to celebrate it.

Io e la mia famiglia festeggiamo il natale in grande stile. Crediamo che il natale sia un periodo per promuovere pace e armonia fra tutti. Diamo il nostro contributo alle organizzazioni. Non siamo solo soldi. Diamo anche vestiti, cibo e tempo. È importante condividerlo con chiunque ne abbia bisogno in questo periodo meraviglioso dell'anno.

My family and I celebrate Christmas in grand fashion with all our friends. We believe that Christmas is a time to promote **peace** and harmony among all. We make our contribution to charities. We do not just give money. We also give clothes, food and **volunteer** our time. It is important to share with everyone who is needy during this wonderful time of the year.

Se vuoi supportare le organizzazioni di carità, cerca coloro che lo fanno nella tua comunità. Ci sono sicuramente organizzazioni che aiutano molte persone. Hanno bisogno di te.

If you want to support charitable organizations, look for those which are **actively** working in your community. Surely there are organizations that are helping many people. They need you.

Per favore rispondi alle seguenti domande.   Please answer the following questions.

Dove si festeggia il natale?   Where is Christmas celebrated?

_____   _____

_____   _____

_____   _____

_____   _____

Cos'è il natale?   What is Christmas?

_____   _____

_____   _____

_____   _____

_____   _____

Per cosa il natale è un'opportunità?   What is Christmas an opportunity for?

_____   _____

_____   _____

_____   _____

_____   _____

Qual è un'altra importante caratteristica del   What is another important characteristic of
natale?   Christmas?

_____   _____

_____   _____

_____   _____

_____   _____

Per chi le organizzazioni fanno buone azioni?	For whom do organizations do positive things?

_____   _____

_____   _____

_____   _____

_____   _____

Come celebriamo il natale io e la mia famiglia?	How do my family and I celebrate Christmas?

_____   _____

_____   _____

_____   _____

_____   _____

Risposte suggerite	Suggested answers

Dove si festeggia il natale?	Where is Christmas celebrated?

Il natale si festeggia in molti Paesi in tutto il mondo.	Christmas is celebrated in many countries around the world.

Cos'è il natale?	What is Christmas?

Il natale è anche una festa di famiglia.

Christmas is also a family celebration.

Per cosa il natale è un'opportunità?

What is Christmas an opportunity for?

Il natale è un'opportunità per dimenticarsi dei problemi e divertirsi con famiglia e amici.

Christmas is an opportunity to forget about problems and have a good time with family and friends.

Qual è un'altra caratteristica importante del natale?

What is another important characteristic of Christmas?

Un'altra caratteristica importante del natale è la generosità.

Another important characteristic of Christmas is generosity.

Per chi le organizzazioni fanno azioni positive?

For whom do organizations do positive things?

Per le persone bisognose.

For poor and needy people.

Come festeggiamo il natale io e la mia famiglia?

How do my family and I celebrate Christmas?

Festeggiamo il natale in grande stile con i nostri amici.

We celebrate Christmas in grand fashion with all of our friends.

Conclusion

W ow! It seems like we just got started and we are already at this point. It has certainly been an interesting trip. We hope that the contents and materials in this book have helped you to improve your overall Italian skills. We are certain that you have put in your best effort in order to do so.

That is why our recommendation is to go back to any of the lessons which you feel you need to review and go over the content. Of course, the more you practice, the better your skills will be. Indeed, your overall skills will improve insofar as you continue to practice.

So, do take this opportunity to continue building on your current skills. You will find that over time, you will progressively gain more and more understanding of the language you encounter on a daily basis.

Give the fact that there are a number of resources out there which can help you to practice your listening skills, such as movies, *telenovelas* and music, you will be able to put this content into practice right away.

Thank you once again for choosing this book. We hope to have met your expectations. And please don't forget to leave a comment. Other folks who are interested in learning Italian will certainly find your reviews on this book useful.

See you in the next level!

CPSIA information can be obtained
at www.ICGtesting.com
Printed in the USA
BVHW092352290121
599087BV00002B/328